Gratitude Journal for Kids

This Journal Belongs To :

....

Be Thankful!

Celebrate your Success!

Share the Joy!

Feel Great Everyday!

WANT FREE GOODIES?!

Email me at
sujatha.lalgudi@gmail.com

Title the email **"Kids Gratitude"** and
I will send some goodies your way!

Thank you
Sujatha Lalgudi

Affirmations

My potential to succeed is infinite.
I take pride in the progress I make each day.
I am proud of myself and all that I have accomplished.
I respect and treat myself with kindness and love.
People like me, and I feel good about myself.
The world is a better place with me in it.
I go for goals with passion and pride.
I am never a burden.
I am worthy of greatness.
I am smart, capable and valuable.
I am at peace with myself.
I accept myself as I am.
I am unique in my own wonderful way.
I am focused, persistent and will never quit.
I am in charge of my own happiness.
I have the power to create change.
I take pride in my achievements.
I have courage and confidence.
I can get through anything.
I don't need to be perfect.
I am an amazing person.
I love myself.
I can do anything.
I can make a difference.
I am in charge of my life.
I set goals and I reach them.
Today, I will walk through my fears.
I am proud of my own success.
I celebrate my individuality.
I am my own superhero.
I am free to be myself.
I trust myself.
I am enough.
I am whole.
I live each day to the fullest.

Day **1**

Date: _____

TODAY I'M GRATEFUL FOR

1. _____

2. _____

3. _____

TODAY WAS AWESOME BECAUSE:
(Draw or Write about it)

The person who brought me joy today:

_____

I FEEL:

Day **2** ⭐

Date: _____

TODAY I'M GRATEFUL FOR

1. _____

2. _____

3. _____

👍👍 TODAY WAS AWESOME BECAUSE: 👍👍
(Draw or Write about it)

I am grateful for this at home:

_____

I FEEL:

Day **3** ⭐

Date: _____

TODAY I'M GRATEFUL FOR

1. _____

2. _____

3. _____

👍👍 **TODAY WAS AWESOME BECAUSE:** 👍👍
(Draw or Write about it)

One thing I appreciate about myself:

_____

I FEEL:

Day **4**

Date: _____

TODAY I'M GRATEFUL FOR

1. _____

2. _____

3. _____

TODAY WAS AWESOME BECAUSE:
(Draw or Write about it)

This person was kind to me today:

_____

I FEEL:

Day **5**

Date: _____

TODAY I'M GRATEFUL FOR

1. _____

2. _____

3. _____

TODAY WAS AWESOME BECAUSE:
(Draw or Write about it)

A book that I enjoyed reading:

_____

I FEEL: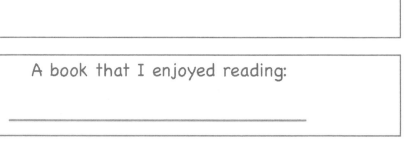

Day **6** ⭐

Date: _____

TODAY I'M GRATEFUL FOR

1. _____

2. _____

3. _____

👍👍 **TODAY WAS AWESOME BECAUSE:** 👍👍
(Draw or Write about it)

It felt great to be helpful to this person:

_____

I FEEL:

Day **7**

Date: _____

TODAY I'M GRATEFUL FOR

1. _____

2. _____

3. _____

 TODAY WAS AWESOME BECAUSE:
(Draw or Write about it)

One thing that made me smile today:

_____

I FEEL:

Congratulations! You completed a week of practicing gratitude.
Use this space to draw, doodle or write your thoughts.

Day **8**

Date: _____

TODAY I'M GRATEFUL FOR

1. _____

2. _____

3. _____

TODAY WAS AWESOME BECAUSE:
(Draw or Write about it)

This cheers me up after a rough day:

_____

I FEEL:

Day **9**

Date: _____

TODAY I'M GRATEFUL FOR

1. _____

2. _____

3. _____

TODAY WAS AWESOME BECAUSE:
(Draw or Write about it)

One skill I learned today:

_____

I FEEL:

Day **10**

Date: _____

TODAY I'M GRATEFUL FOR

1. _____

2. _____

3. _____

TODAY WAS AWESOME BECAUSE:
(Draw or Write about it)

Something that made me laugh today:

_____

I FEEL:

Day **11** ⭐

Date: _____

TODAY I'M GRATEFUL FOR

1. _____

2. _____

3. _____

👍👍 **TODAY WAS AWESOME BECAUSE:** 👍👍
(Draw or Write about it)

Someone who helps me to stay healthy:

_____

I FEEL:

Day **12** ⭐

Date: _____

TODAY I'M GRATEFUL FOR

1. _____

2. _____

3. _____

👍👍 TODAY WAS AWESOME BECAUSE: 👍👍
(Draw or Write about it)

I am so glad that I am very good at:

_____

I FEEL:

Day **13**

Date: _____

TODAY I'M GRATEFUL FOR

1. _____

2. _____

3. _____

 TODAY WAS AWESOME BECAUSE:
(Draw or Write about it)

A place that I like to visit:

_____

I FEEL:

Day **14**

Date: _____

1. _____

2. _____

3. _____

TODAY WAS AWESOME BECAUSE:
(Draw or Write about it)

A Favorite thing I like about my school:

_____

I FEEL:

Congratulations! You completed a week of practicing gratitude.
Use this space to draw, doodle or write your thoughts.

Day **15**

Date: _____

TODAY I'M GRATEFUL FOR

1. _____

2. _____

3. _____

TODAY WAS AWESOME BECAUSE:
(Draw or Write about it)

An unexpected surprise today:

_____

I FEEL:

Day **16** ⭐

Date: _____

TODAY I'M GRATEFUL FOR

1. _____

2. _____

3. _____

👍👍 **TODAY WAS AWESOME BECAUSE:** 👍👍
(Draw or Write about it)

Holiday I am thankful for:

_____

I FEEL:

Day **17**

Date: _____

TODAY I'M GRATEFUL FOR

1. _____

2. _____

3. _____

TODAY WAS AWESOME BECAUSE:
(Draw or Write about it)

My favorite thing about this season:

_____

I FEEL:

Day **18**

Date: _____

TODAY I'M GRATEFUL FOR

1. _____

2. _____

3. _____

 TODAY WAS AWESOME BECAUSE:
(Draw or Write about it)

I am grateful for this at home:

_____

I FEEL: 😦   😠

Day **19**

Date: _____

TODAY I'M GRATEFUL FOR

1. _____

2. _____

3. _____

TODAY WAS AWESOME BECAUSE:
(Draw or Write about it)

A wonderful experience I had recently:

_____

I FEEL:

Day **20**

Date: _____

TODAY I'M GRATEFUL FOR

1. _____

2. _____

3. _____

TODAY WAS AWESOME BECAUSE:
(Draw or Write about it)

Something I was putting off but finally got it done:

_____

I FEEL:

Day **21**

Date: _____

TODAY I'M GRATEFUL FOR

1. _____

2. _____

3. _____

TODAY WAS AWESOME BECAUSE:
(Draw or Write about it)

A gift I am grateful for:

_____

I FEEL:

Congratulations! You completed a week of practicing gratitude.
Use this space to draw, doodle or write your thoughts.

Day **22**

Date: _____

TODAY I'M GRATEFUL FOR

1. _____

2. _____

3. _____

TODAY WAS AWESOME BECAUSE:
(Draw or Write about it)

One thing that makes my life easier:

_____

I FEEL:

Day **23**

Date: _____

TODAY I'M GRATEFUL FOR

1. _____

2. _____

3. _____

TODAY WAS AWESOME BECAUSE:
(Draw or Write about it)

Singing this song makes me happy:

_____

I FEEL:

Day **24**

Date: _____

TODAY I'M GRATEFUL FOR

1. _____

2. _____

3. _____

TODAY WAS AWESOME BECAUSE:
(Draw or Write about it)

Something nice I did for someone today:

_____

I FEEL:

Day **25**

Date: _____

TODAY I'M GRATEFUL FOR

1. _____

2. _____

3. _____

TODAY WAS AWESOME BECAUSE:
(Draw or Write about it)

A friend I enjoyed playing with today:

_____

I FEEL:

Day **26**

Date: _____

TODAY I'M GRATEFUL FOR

1. _____

2. _____

3. _____

TODAY WAS AWESOME BECAUSE:
(Draw or Write about it)

One way I have bettered myself recently:

_____

I FEEL:

Day **27**

Date: _____

TODAY I'M GRATEFUL FOR

1. _____

2. _____

3. _____

 TODAY WAS AWESOME BECAUSE:
(Draw or Write about it)

A recent dish I loved eating:

_____

I FEEL:

Day **28**

Date: _____

TODAY I'M GRATEFUL FOR

1. _____

2. _____

3. _____

TODAY WAS AWESOME BECAUSE:
(Draw or Write about it)

One thing I appreciate in nature:

_____

I FEEL:

Congratulations! You completed a week of practicing gratitude.
Use this space to draw, doodle or write your thoughts.

Day **29**

Date: _____

TODAY I'M GRATEFUL FOR

1. _____

2. _____

3. _____

TODAY WAS AWESOME BECAUSE:
(Draw or Write about it)

It felt great to be helpful to this person:

_____

I FEEL:

Day **30**

Date: _____

TODAY I'M GRATEFUL FOR

1. _____

2. _____

3. _____

TODAY WAS AWESOME BECAUSE:
(Draw or Write about it)

One thing that I wear that makes me feel good:

_____

I FEEL:

Day **31**

TODAY I'M GRATEFUL FOR

1. _____

2. _____

3. _____

TODAY WAS AWESOME BECAUSE:
(Draw or Write about it)

Singing this song makes me happy:

_____

I FEEL:

Day **32**

Date: _____

TODAY I'M GRATEFUL FOR

1. _____

2. _____

3. _____

TODAY WAS AWESOME BECAUSE:
(Draw or Write about it)

One thing that helps me relax:

_____

I FEEL:

Day **33**

Date: _____

TODAY I'M GRATEFUL FOR

1. _____

2. _____

3. _____

TODAY WAS AWESOME BECAUSE:
(Draw or Write about it)

One thing I am grateful for that helps me travel:

_____

I FEEL:

Day **34**

Date: _____

TODAY I'M GRATEFUL FOR

1. _____

2. _____

3. _____

TODAY WAS AWESOME BECAUSE:
(Draw or Write about it)

Someone who inspired me:

_____

I FEEL:

Day **35**

Date: _____

TODAY I'M GRATEFUL FOR

1. _____

2. _____

3. _____

TODAY WAS AWESOME BECAUSE:
(Draw or Write about it)

Something that cheers me up after a tiring day:

_____

I FEEL:

Congratulations! You completed a week of practicing gratitude.
Use this space to draw, doodle or write your thoughts.

Day **36**

Date: _____

TODAY I'M GRATEFUL FOR

1. _____

2. _____

3. _____

TODAY WAS AWESOME BECAUSE:
(Draw or Write about it)

Something that keeps me warm:

_____

I FEEL:

Day **37**

Date: _____

TODAY I'M GRATEFUL FOR

1. _____

2. _____

3. _____

TODAY WAS AWESOME BECAUSE:
(Draw or Write about it)

The person who brought me joy today:

_____

I FEEL:

Day **38**

Date: _____

TODAY I'M GRATEFUL FOR

1. _____

2. _____

3. _____

TODAY WAS AWESOME BECAUSE:
(Draw or Write about it)

My favorite activity today:

_____

I FEEL:

Day **39**

Date: _____

TODAY I'M GRATEFUL FOR

1. _____

2. _____

3. _____

TODAY WAS AWESOME BECAUSE:
(Draw or Write about it)

One thing I appreciate about myself:

_____

I FEEL:

Day **40**

Date: _____

TODAY I'M GRATEFUL FOR

1. _____

2. _____

3. _____

 TODAY WAS AWESOME BECAUSE:
(Draw or Write about it)

This person was kind to me today:

_____

I FEEL:

Day **41**

TODAY I'M GRATEFUL FOR

Date: _____

1. _____

2. _____

3. _____

TODAY WAS AWESOME BECAUSE:
(Draw or Write about it)

A book that I enjoyed reading:

_____

I FEEL:

Day **42**

Date: _____

TODAY I'M GRATEFUL FOR

1. _____

2. _____

3. _____

TODAY WAS AWESOME BECAUSE:
(Draw or Write about it)

One thing that made me smile today:

_____

I FEEL:

Congratulations! You completed a week of practicing gratitude.
Use this space to draw, doodle or write your thoughts.

Day **43**

Date: _____

TODAY I'M GRATEFUL FOR

1. _____

2. _____

3. _____

 TODAY WAS AWESOME BECAUSE:
(Draw or Write about it)

This cheers me up after a rough day:

_____

I FEEL:

Day **44**

Date: _____

TODAY I'M GRATEFUL FOR

1. _____

2. _____

3. _____

TODAY WAS AWESOME BECAUSE:
(Draw or Write about it)

One skill I learned today:

_____

I FEEL:

Day **45**

Date: _____

TODAY I'M GRATEFUL FOR

1. _____

2. _____

3. _____

TODAY WAS AWESOME BECAUSE:
(Draw or Write about it)

Something that made me laugh today:

_____

I FEEL:

Day **46**

Date: _____

TODAY I'M GRATEFUL FOR

1. _____

2. _____

3. _____

TODAY WAS AWESOME BECAUSE:
(Draw or Write about it)

Someone who helps me to stay healthy:

_____

I FEEL:

Day **47**

Date: _____

TODAY I'M GRATEFUL FOR

1. _____

2. _____

3. _____

TODAY WAS AWESOME BECAUSE:
(Draw or Write about it)

I am so glad that I am very good at:

_____

I FEEL:

Day **48**

Date: _____

TODAY I'M GRATEFUL FOR

1. _____

2. _____

3. _____

TODAY WAS AWESOME BECAUSE:
(Draw or Write about it)

A place that I like to visit:

_____

I FEEL: 😄 🙂 😐 🙁 😠

Day **49**

Date: _____

TODAY I'M GRATEFUL FOR

1. _____

2. _____

3. _____

TODAY WAS AWESOME BECAUSE:
(Draw or Write about it)

A Favorite thing I like about my school:

_____

I FEEL:

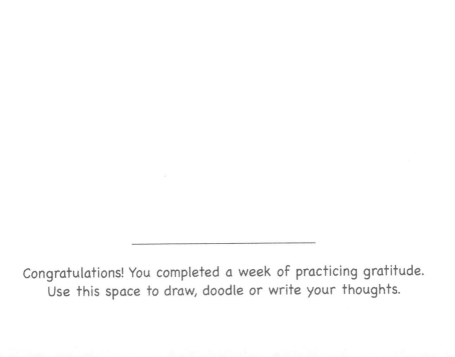

Congratulations! You completed a week of practicing gratitude.
Use this space to draw, doodle or write your thoughts.

Day **50**

Date: _____

TODAY I'M GRATEFUL FOR

1. _____

2. _____

3. _____

TODAY WAS AWESOME BECAUSE:
(Draw or Write about it)

An unexpected surprise today:

_____

I FEEL:

Day **51**

Date: _____

TODAY I'M GRATEFUL FOR

1. _____

2. _____

3. _____

TODAY WAS AWESOME BECAUSE:
(Draw or Write about it)

Holiday I am thankful for:

_____

I FEEL:

Day **52**

Date: _____

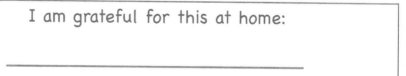
TODAY I'M GRATEFUL FOR

1. _____

2. _____

3. _____

TODAY WAS AWESOME BECAUSE:
(Draw or Write about it)

I am grateful for this at home:

_____

I FEEL:

Day **53**

Date: _____

1. _____

2. _____

3. _____

TODAY WAS AWESOME BECAUSE:
(Draw or Write about it)

A wonderful experience I had recently:

_____

I FEEL:

Day **54**

Date: _____

TODAY I'M GRATEFUL FOR

1. _____

2. _____

3. _____

TODAY WAS AWESOME BECAUSE:
(Draw or Write about it)

Something I was putting off but finally got it done:

_____

I FEEL:

Day **55**

Date: _____

TODAY I'M GRATEFUL FOR

1. _____

2. _____

3. _____

TODAY WAS AWESOME BECAUSE:
(Draw or Write about it)

A gift I am grateful for:

_____

I FEEL:

Day **56**

Date: _____

TODAY I'M GRATEFUL FOR

1. _____

2. _____

3. _____

TODAY WAS AWESOME BECAUSE:
(Draw or Write about it)

One thing that makes my life easier:

_____

I FEEL:

Congratulations! You completed a week of practicing gratitude.
Use this space to draw, doodle or write your thoughts.

Day **57**

Date: _____

TODAY I'M GRATEFUL FOR

1. _____

2. _____

3. _____

TODAY WAS AWESOME BECAUSE:
(Draw or Write about it)

A book that I enjoyed reading:

_____

I FEEL:

Day **58**

Date: _____

1. _____

2. _____

3. _____

TODAY WAS AWESOME BECAUSE:
(Draw or Write about it)

Something nice I did for someone today:

_____

I FEEL: 😃 🙂 😐 🙁 😠

Day **59**

Date: _____

TODAY I'M GRATEFUL FOR

1. _____

2. _____

3. _____

TODAY WAS AWESOME BECAUSE:
(Draw or Write about it)

A friend I enjoyed playing with today:

_____

I FEEL:

Day 60

Date: _____

TODAY I'M GRATEFUL FOR

1. _____

2. _____

3. _____

TODAY WAS AWESOME BECAUSE:
(Draw or Write about it)

One way I have bettered myself recently:

_____

I FEEL: 😃 🙂 😐 🙁 😠

Day **61**

Date: _____

TODAY I'M GRATEFUL FOR

1. _____

2. _____

3. _____

TODAY WAS AWESOME BECAUSE:
(Draw or Write about it)

A recent dish I loved eating:

_____

I FEEL:

Day **62**

Date: _____

1. _____

2. _____

3. _____

TODAY WAS AWESOME BECAUSE:
(Draw or Write about it)

One thing I appreciate in nature:

_____

I FEEL:

Day **63**

Date: _____

1. _____

2. _____

3. _____

TODAY WAS AWESOME BECAUSE:
(Draw or Write about it)

The person who brought me joy today:

_____

I FEEL:

_____

Congratulations! You completed a week of practicing gratitude.
Use this space to draw, doodle or write your thoughts.

Day **64**

Date: _____

TODAY I'M GRATEFUL FOR

1. _____

2. _____

3. _____

TODAY WAS AWESOME BECAUSE:
(Draw or Write about it)

It felt great to be helpful to this person:

_____

I FEEL:

Day **65**

Date: _____

TODAY I'M GRATEFUL FOR

1. _____

2. _____

3. _____

TODAY WAS AWESOME BECAUSE:
(Draw or Write about it)

One thing that I wear that makes me feel good:

_____

I FEEL:

Day **66**

Date: _____

TODAY I'M GRATEFUL FOR

1. _____

2. _____

3. _____

TODAY WAS AWESOME BECAUSE:
(Draw or Write about it)

Singing this song makes me happy:

_____

I FEEL:

Day **67**

Date: _____

TODAY I'M GRATEFUL FOR

1. _____

2. _____

3. _____

TODAY WAS AWESOME BECAUSE:
(Draw or Write about it)

One thing that helps me relax:

_____

I FEEL:

Day **68**

Date: _____

TODAY I'M GRATEFUL FOR

1. _____

2. _____

3. _____

TODAY WAS AWESOME BECAUSE:
(Draw or Write about it)

Someone who inspired me:

_____

I FEEL:

Day **69**

Date: _____

TODAY I'M GRATEFUL FOR

1. _____

2. _____

3. _____

TODAY WAS AWESOME BECAUSE:
(Draw or Write about it)

Something that cheers me up after a tiring day:

_____

I FEEL:

Day **70**

Date: _____

TODAY I'M GRATEFUL FOR

1. _____

2. _____

3. _____

TODAY WAS AWESOME BECAUSE:
(Draw or Write about it)

My favorite thing about this season:

_____

I FEEL:

Congratulations! You completed a week of practicing gratitude.
Use this space to draw, doodle or write your thoughts.

Day **71**

Date: _____

TODAY I'M GRATEFUL FOR

1. _____

2. _____

3. _____

TODAY WAS AWESOME BECAUSE:
(Draw or Write about it)

The person who brought me joy today:

_____

I FEEL:

Day **72**

Date: _____

TODAY I'M GRATEFUL FOR

1. _____

2. _____

3. _____

TODAY WAS AWESOME BECAUSE:
(Draw or Write about it)

Something that keeps me warm:

_____

I FEEL:

Day **73**

Date: _____

TODAY I'M GRATEFUL FOR

1. _____

2. _____

3. _____

TODAY WAS AWESOME BECAUSE:
(Draw or Write about it)

One thing I am grateful for that helps me travel:

_____

I FEEL:

Day **74**

Date: _____

1. _____

2. _____

3. _____

TODAY WAS AWESOME BECAUSE:
(Draw or Write about it)

Something that made me laugh today:

_____

I FEEL:

Day **75**

Date: _____

TODAY I'M GRATEFUL FOR

1. _____

2. _____

3. _____

TODAY WAS AWESOME BECAUSE:
(Draw or Write about it)

One thing I appreciate about myself:

_____

I FEEL:

Day **76**

Date: _____

TODAY I'M GRATEFUL FOR

1. _____

2. _____

3. _____

TODAY WAS AWESOME BECAUSE:
(Draw or Write about it)

This person was kind to me today:

_____

I FEEL:

Day **77**

Date: _____

TODAY I'M GRATEFUL FOR

1. _____

2. _____

3. _____

TODAY WAS AWESOME BECAUSE:
(Draw or Write about it)

Something nice I did for someone today:

_____

I FEEL:

Congratulations! You completed a week of practicing gratitude.
Use this space to draw, doodle or write your thoughts.

Day **78**

Date: _____

TODAY I'M GRATEFUL FOR

1. _____

2. _____

3. _____

 TODAY WAS AWESOME BECAUSE:
(Draw or Write about it)

A book that I enjoyed reading:

_____

I FEEL:

Day **79**

Date: _____

1. _____

2. _____

3. _____

TODAY WAS AWESOME BECAUSE:
(Draw or Write about it)

One thing that made me smile today:

_____

I FEEL: 😊   🙂   😐   🙁   😠

Day **80**

Date: _____

TODAY I'M GRATEFUL FOR

1. _____

2. _____

3. _____

TODAY WAS AWESOME BECAUSE:
(Draw or Write about it)

This cheers me up after a rough day:

_____

I FEEL:

Day **81**

Date: _____

TODAY I'M GRATEFUL FOR

1. _____

2. _____

3. _____

👍👍 **TODAY WAS AWESOME BECAUSE:**
(Draw or Write about it) 👍👍

One skill I learned today:

_____

I FEEL: 😠

Day **82**

Date: _____

TODAY I'M GRATEFUL FOR

1. _____

2. _____

3. _____

TODAY WAS AWESOME BECAUSE:
(Draw or Write about it)

Something that made me laugh today:

_____

I FEEL:

Day **83**

Date: _____

TODAY I'M GRATEFUL FOR

1. _____

2. _____

3. _____

TODAY WAS AWESOME BECAUSE:
(Draw or Write about it)

I am so glad that I am very good at:

_____

I FEEL:

Day **84**

Date: _____

TODAY I'M GRATEFUL FOR

1. _____

2. _____

3. _____

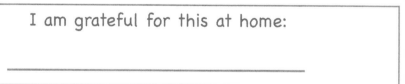

TODAY WAS AWESOME BECAUSE:
(Draw or Write about it)

I am grateful for this at home:

_____

I FEEL:

Congratulations! You completed a week of practicing gratitude.
Use this space to draw, doodle or write your thoughts.

Day **85**

Date: _____

TODAY I'M GRATEFUL FOR

1. _____

2. _____

3. _____

TODAY WAS AWESOME BECAUSE:
(Draw or Write about it)

Something I was putting off but finally got it done:

_____

I FEEL:

Day **86**

Date: _____

TODAY I'M GRATEFUL FOR

1. _____

2. _____

3. _____

 TODAY WAS AWESOME BECAUSE:
(Draw or Write about it)

Something nice I did for someone today:

_____

I FEEL:

Day **87**

Date: _____

TODAY I'M GRATEFUL FOR

1. _____

2. _____

3. _____

TODAY WAS AWESOME BECAUSE:
(Draw or Write about it)

One way I have bettered myself recently:

_____

I FEEL:

Day **88**

Date: _____

1. _____

2. _____

3. _____

TODAY WAS AWESOME BECAUSE:
(Draw or Write about it)

It felt great to be helpful to this person:

_____

I FEEL:

Day **89**

Date: _____

TODAY I'M GRATEFUL FOR

1. _____

2. _____

3. _____

TODAY WAS AWESOME BECAUSE:
(Draw or Write about it)

One skill I learned today:

_____

I FEEL:

Day **90**

Date: _____

TODAY I'M GRATEFUL FOR

1. _____

2. _____

3. _____

TODAY WAS AWESOME BECAUSE:
(Draw or Write about it)

The person who brought me joy today:

_____

I FEEL:

Congratulations! You completed a week of practicing gratitude.
Use this space to draw, doodle or write your thoughts.

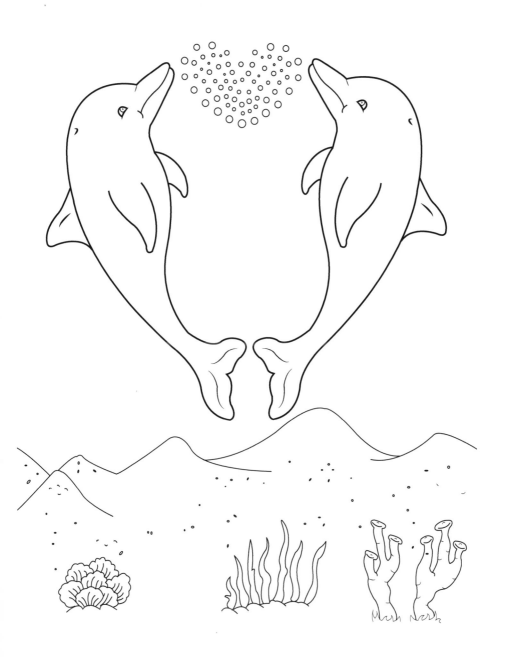

Use this coloring space to color, relax and reflect.

Make Gratitude your new habit

As you practice your new habit each day,

Celebrate your progress and check off each day of your efforts!

Week 1	1	2	3	4	5	6	7	1
Week 2	8	9	10	11	12	13	14	2
Week 3	15	16	17	18	19	20	21	3
Week 4	22	23	24	25	26	27	28	4
Week 5	29	30	31	32	33	34	35	5
Week 6	36	37	38	39	40	41	42	6
Week 7	43	44	45	46	47	48	49	7
Week 8	50	51	52	53	54	55	56	8
Week 9	57	58	59	60	61	62	63	9
Week 10	64	65	66	67	68	69	70	10
Week 11	71	72	73	74	75	76	77	11
Week 12	78	79	80	81	82	83	84	12
Week 13	85	86	87	88	89	90		13

.

Made in the USA
Monee, IL
16 October 2022

15964913R00061